USERNAME: **REGENERATED**

MINDY LOPKIN IS RESPONSIBLE FOR ALL THE COOL SPEECH BUBBLES, EFFECTS AND LETTERING.

AMRIT BIRDI IS THE GUY BEHIND THE INCREDIBLE ILLUSTRATIONS IN THE USERNAME SERIES.

JOE SUGG CREATED THE STORYLINE AND CHARACTERS AND DIRECTED THE PROJECT TO MAKE THE BEST GRAPHIC NOVEL SERIES POSSIBLE.

MATT WHYMAN IS THE PERSON WHO TOOK THE STORY AND CREATED A GRIPPING NARRATIVE TO ACCOMPANY THE ARTWORK.

JOAQUIN PEREYRA BROUGHT THE IMAGES TO LIFE WITH HIS AMAZING COLOURING.

TO EVERY KEITH I'VE EVER MET
OR WILL MEET IN THE FUTURE...
CURRENTLY ON ZERO.

USERNAME:
REGENERATED

JOE SUGG

HODDER &
STOUGHTON

First published in Great Britain in 2016 by Hodder & Stoughton
An Hachette UK company

1

Copyright © Joe Sugg, 2016
With thanks to Matt Whyman
Artwork produced by Amrit Birdi & Co
Illustrator: Amrit Birdi
Colours: Jaoquin Pereyra
Letters: Mindy Lopkin
Art Assistant: Lisamaria Laxholm

A CIP catalogue record for this title is available from the British Library

Hardback ISBN 9781473636941
Trade Paperback 9781473636958
eBook ISBN 9781473636965

Printed and bound in Italy by Graphicom S.r.l

Hodder & Stoughton policy is to use papers that are natural, renewable and recyclable products and made from wood grown in sustainable forests. The logging and manufacturing processes are expected to conform to the environmental regulations of the country of origin.

Hodder & Stoughton Ltd
Carmelite House
50 Victoria Embankment
London EC4Y 0DZ

www.hodder.co.uk

HELLO AGAIN

I NEVER QUITE THOUGHT I WOULD BE SAYING THIS BUT HERE IT IS..! BOOK TWO IN THE USERNAME SERIES! AND JUST LIKE THE LAST TIME I'M SO EXCITED FOR YOU TO READ AND ENJOY THE STORY AND LET ME KNOW WHAT YOU THINK.

ONCE AGAIN I HAVE YOU GUYS TO THANK FOR MAKING THIS POSSIBLE. YOU MIGHT BE WONDERING, 'JOSEPH, WERE YOU SURPRISED BY THE SUCCESS OF YOUR FIRST GRAPHIC NOVEL, USERNAME: EVIE?', AND THE ANSWER IS, 'YES I FLIPPIN' WELL WAS!'. I'VE BEEN OVERWHELMED BY JUST HOW AMAZING THE RESPONSE WAS – FROM REVIEWS ONLINE, THE REACTION TO SIGNINGS (I MET OVER 5,000 OF YOU) AND COMMENTS ACROSS MY CHANNELS. I STILL CAN'T BELIEVE EVERYTHING WE'VE ACHIEVED TOGETHER WITH USERNAME: EVIE.

BUT WHAT WAS EVEN BETTER TO ME WAS THAT SO MANY OF YOU HAVE SAID USERNAME:EVIE WAS THE FIRST GRAPHIC NOVEL YOU'D READ AND HOW MUCH YOU HAD ENJOYED THIS KIND OF BOOK, WHICH WAS REALLY IMPORTANT TO ME RIGHT FROM THE START. AS YOU KNOW I'VE ALWAYS BEEN INTO COMICS AND GRAPHIC NOVELS SINCE WAY BACK AND TO INTRODUCE NEW READERS TO THE GENRE IS SOMETHING I NEVER EXPECTED BUT AM SO PROUD OF. YOU LOT ARE THE BEST AND I'M SO HAPPY YOU ENJOYED EVIE'S FIRST ADVENTURE.

QUESTION IS ARE YOU READY FOR THE NEXT ONE?

SO WHAT CAN YOU EXPECT FROM USERNAME: REGENERATED? WELL FOR A START THERE'S PLENTY OF FAMILIAR FACES, BUT TIME HAS PASSED AND ALTHOUGH YOU MIGHT RECOGNISE THE GANG FROM U:E (THAT'S A HANDY ABBREVIATION ISN'T IT?) THEY'VE DEFINITELY DONE A LOT OF GROWING UP. AND OF COURSE THERE'S A WHOLE CAST OF NEW CHARACTERS FOR YOU TO GET TO KNOW. THERE'S ADVENTURE, DANGER, EVEN REVISITING THE PAST! UNEXPECTED FRIENDSHIPS AND A TWISTY PLOT TO KEEP YOU ON YOUR TOES.

I'VE LIVED WITH THESE CHARACTERS SINCE WAY BACK BEFORE EVEN THE RELEASE OF U:E AND FOR THIS BOOK I REALLY WANTED TO DEVELOP THEM AND THEIR STORIES – GIVING THEM MORE DEPTH AND SHOWING DIFFERENT SIDES TO THEM AND THEIR WORLD (OR SHOULD THAT BE WORLDS). AND I'LL LET YOU INTO A LITTLE SECRET... I'D ALWAYS IMAGINED THERE TO BE MORE THAN ONE BOOK SO WHAT YOU'RE ABOUT TO READ IS LIKE ANOTHER EPISODE IN THE USERNAME SERIES!

ONCE AGAIN THANKS TO EVERY ONE OF YOU WHO TAKES THE TIME OUT TO WATCH MY VIDEOS, READ MY BOOKS AND SUPPORT ALL THE AMAZING THINGS I GET TO DO. I HOPE YOU GET AS MUCH OUT OF THE THINGS I MAKE AS I DO CREATING THEM. YOU LOT ARE MY BIGGEST INSPIRATION AND NONE OF THIS WOULD BE POSSIBLE WITHOUT YOU – THANKS FOR COMING ON THIS CRAZY RIDE WITH ME.

SO SIT BACK, RELAX, AND ENJOY THE RIDE THAT IS USERNAME: REGENERATED.

ALL THE BEST

JOE

1

2

3

6

MAYBE YOU'D LIKE TO SETTLE EVIE IN HER COT. THAT'S IF YOU CAN REMEMBER WHERE THE NURSERY IS.

HONEY, WHAT ELSE CAN I SAY? IT WAS A BIG MOMENT FOR ME... A BIG MOMENT FOR US ALL.

I STARTED WORK ON E.SCAPE THE DAY OUR DAUGHTER WAS BORN, AND NOW IT'S READY TO GO LIVE. ALL I WANT TO DO IS CREATE A PLACE SHE CAN CALL HER OWN WHEN SHE'S OLDER.

A SANCTUARY, IF YOU LIKE, TO GET AWAY FROM THE STRESSES OF THIS WORLD AND RECHARGE.

BUT IT'S JUST A STRING OF CODE.

OH, IT'S SO MUCH MORE THAN THAT.

E.SCAPE IS YEARS AHEAD OF ITS TIME.

A VIRTUAL WORLD THAT FEELS COMPLETELY REAL. IT'S PROGRAMMED TO REFLECT EVIE'S PERSONALITY AND CONNECT WITH HER IN EVERY WAY.

THE LANDSCAPE MIGHT BE A LITTLE BASIC RIGHT NOW, BUT BY SAMPLING HER PRESENCE IT'LL BEGIN TO EVOLVE TO SUIT HER PERSONALITY.

BY THE TIME EVIE'S OLD ENOUGH TO FEEL THE NEED FOR SOME TIME AND SPACE TO HERSELF, SHE'LL HAVE A PERSONAL PARADISE!

OR A USELESS REMINDER OF HOW HER CRAZY FATHER TURNED HIS BACK ON THE FIRST YEAR OF HER LIFE.

17

THE HABITAT SYSTEM SEEMS STABLE. NO GLITCHES OR BUGS REPORTED.

SO, IT CAN ONLY BE A PROBLEM WITH... THE GATEWAY.

FFSSSHHHH

PLEASE TELL ME YOU'RE SAFE ON THE OTHER SIDE. GIVE ME A SIGN. **ANYTHING!** HONEY...

❌ GATEWAY ERROR

FFSSSHHHH

FFSSSHHHH

I'M SORRY. SO SORRY!

PART ONE

RIGHT NOW

THEY COME AS I SLEEP...

... AND BREAK INTO MY DREAMS.

WHEN I OPEN MY EYES, THEY'RE GONE.

ONCE UPON A TIME, SUCH A PLACE WAS JUST A MOUSE CLICK AWAY.

NOW, BOTH MY DAD AND THE SANCTUARY HE CREATED ARE HISTORY.

I'M SO TIRED OF THESE NIGHTMARES.

WHAT I NEED IS SOME PLACE I CAN GO TO GET AWAY FROM IT ALL.

EVIE:
E.SCAPE ESCAPEE. RESTLESS SOUL.

SHHRIP

INCLUDING EVERYONE IN IT.

I THINK ABOUT YOU SO MUCH, BUT NEVER KNEW YOUR NAME.

YOU SACRIFICED YOURSELF SO I COULD COME BACK. BUT IT DOESN'T FEEL LIKE HOME WITHOUT YOU.

IF I COULD RETURN TO E.SCAPE, I'D GO IN A HEARTBEAT. BUT WHEN DAD SHUT DOWN THAT WORLD TO START IT AFRESH, JUST MOMENTS AFTER I GOT OUT, IT COOKED SOMETHING IN THE SOFTWARE.

I CAN STILL LOOK IN...

E.SCAPE

BRRK

... BUT ONLY FROM AFAR, IT SEEMS.

I CAN'T WALK THROUGH THE GLADES, BREATHE THE FRESH AIR OR EXPERIENCE THE FREEDOM DAD CREATED FOR ME.

THAT CONNECTION HAS GONE, ALONG WITH MY FATHER...

... AND I MISS IT MADLY.

IT'S A GREAT WAY TO GET IN TOUCH WITH STRONG EMOTIONS, RIGHT? A CRUSH CAN MAKE YOU FEEL GOOD AT TIMES, BUT WHEN THAT PERSON IS LITERALLY BEYOND YOUR REACH...

... WELL, THAT'S WHEN IT BECOMES MORE LIKE A CURSE. AND TIME YOU TURNED TO YOUR FAVOURITE COUSIN FOR A CURE.

I KIND OF OWE YOU, SEEING THAT IT WAS ME WHO MADE A MESS OF YOUR LITTLE PIXEL PLAYGROUND.

BUT OUR E.SCAPE ADVENTURE OPENED MY EYES TO A FEW THINGS.

POP

SO, WHAT DO YOU SUGGEST?

FIRSTLY, WALK AWAY FROM YOUR LAPTOP AND GET REAL.

IT'S TIME TO EMBRACE LIFE, EVIE.

AND THAT CAN START BY MAKING THE MOST OF PROM NIGHT.

LIONEL WOULD THINK HE'D WON THE *LOTTERY* IF YOU ASKED HIM TO BE YOUR DATE.

LIONEL IS LOVELY, BUT HE'S JUST A LITTLE... *INTENSE.*

IF YOU'RE NOT INTO HIM, THEN YOU SHOULD LET HIM KNOW.

♪DIDDLE DAH DAH♪ ♪DIDDLE DAH DAH-DEE♪

AND BREAK HIS LITTLE HEART?

29

MALLORY, THAT WOULD JUST MAKE ME FEEL WORSE.

LIONEL

BLAP

ALL YOU'RE DOING IS FEEDING THIS DAYDREAM THAT YOUR HOODED HERO WILL MAKE EVERYTHING BETTER.

WE ALL KNOW IT'S BEEN TOUGH FOR YOU LATELY, BUT DON'T LOSE SIGHT OF THE GOOD THINGS YOU'VE GOT GOING HERE.

LIKE ME, FOR STARTERS.

IT'S ALL ABOUT MAKING THE EFFORT, AND CREATING A GOOD TIME RATHER THAN THINKING YOU'RE MISSING OUT ON A BETTER ONE.

WE CAN'T ALL STRIKE LUCKY AND DATE HOT, RIPPED GUYS, RIGHT?

HOW IS JASPAR?

I'M ABOUT TO DROP ROUND AND FIND OUT.

LET'S HOPE HE LIKES MY NEW LOOK.

THERE'LL BE TROUBLE IF HE DOESN'T.

TOO RIGHT!

THINK ABOUT WHAT I SAID, EVIE.

A CRUSH CAN BE FUN, UNTIL IT BECOMES A MONSTER.

THEN IT'S TIME TO GET A GRIP.

MALLORY WAS RIGHT. BUT HOW COULD I JUST SHUT DOWN ON THIS GUY? BACK IN E.SCAPE, HE HAD BEEN THERE FOR ME WHEN I NEEDED HIS HELP.

SWITCHING OFF JUST WASN'T AN OPTION.

BRKK BLIP BRKK

NOT WITHOUT A PROPER GOODBYE.

I'D LOST COUNT OF THE TIMES I'D TRIED TO RETURN.

ON EVERY OCCASION, I'D FIND MYSELF THERE...

BRKK BRKK

BUT NOT THERE.

EVEN THOUGH I COULDN'T CROSS OVER FOR REAL...

... IT ALWAYS HELPED ME TO FEEL CLOSER TO HIM.

HERE WAS A WORLD THAT HAD BEEN GIVEN A FRESH START. A PARADISE LOST, BUT CODED TO REGENERATE JUST FOR ME.

EVERY VIRTUAL ATOM WAS PROGRAMMED TO PICK UP ON MY PRESENCE, AND YET SOMETHING IN THIS PROGRAM HAD BROKEN.

SOMETHING THAT STOPPED ME FROM TRULY CONNECTING.

IN THE YEAR SINCE I'D SCRAMBLED FROM E.SCAPE, ALL I COULD DO WAS LOOK BACK IN FROM A DISTANCE.

DAD'S REBOOT HAD LAID WASTE TO A CORRUPTED LAND, AND YET I HELD OUT HOPE THAT THE VIRTUAL SOUL MATE I FOUND HERE WOULD BE WAITING FOR ME.

NOW MALLORY HAD BROUGHT HOME JUST WHAT THIS WAS DOING TO MY HEART AS MUCH AS MY HEAD. IT WAS TIME TO GET REAL.

TO OVERCOME THESE FEELINGS, I HAVE TO ACCEPT HE'S GONE.

AND IT'S NOT LIKE I'M A STRANGER TO LOSS.

MUM LEFT US LONG AGO.

SHE GOT ILL. THAT'S ALL DAD EVER SAID.

IT HAUNTED HIM FOR SURE, BUT HE'S IN A BETTER PLACE NOW.

MALLORY AND HER FAMILY HAVE BEEN GOOD TO ME SINCE THEN, BUT THE FUTURE IS IN MY HANDS.

GASP

EVIE, IT'S TIME TO START LIVING AGAIN!

EVIE, FANCY BUMPING INTO YOU!

MUST BE THE FIFTH TIME IN ONE DAY, LIONEL.

WHAT ARE THE CHANCES?

HMM... LET ME SEE, OVER A SIX-HOUR PERIOD, WITH 2000 STUDENTS IN A BUILDING THAT MEASURES...

I DIDN'T MEAN IT LITERALLY.

SO, WHAT'VE YOU BEEN UP TO IN THE HALF HOUR SINCE I LAST SAW YOU?

SWEET.

I JUST SCORED 98% IN COMPUTER SCIENCE, WHICH IS FRUSTRATING, BUT...

... WELL, I'M WORRIED ABOUT YOU, EVIE.

MY HEAD TELLS ME TO WALK AWAY.

IF MY HEART IS WRONG HERE, I'M DEAD AGAIN.

GRAAAGGHHH

BUT YOU SOUND LIKE YOU'RE IN PAIN, AND I CAN'T IGNORE THAT.

THE WAY I SEE THINGS, IT ALL COMES DOWN TO TRUST. I SET YOU FREE. YOU CONTROL YOUR INSTINCT TO CRUSH MY SKULL. DO WE HAVE A DEAL?

MURHH.

GOOD!

UNLESS THAT GRUNT IS A NO?

I GUESS THERE'S ONLY ONE WAY TO FIND OUT.

JUST HANG IN THERE BIG GUY AND CHILL OUT. SERIOUSLY.

GRAGEHH

IT'S ALL ABOUT TEAMWORK, OAK, OLD BUDDY.

INSTEAD OF GOING TO WAR, WE'VE CREATED SOMETHING HERE THAT NEITHER OF US COULD'VE ACHIEVED ON OUR OWN.

WHO KNEW A BRUTE LIKE YOU COULD BUILD SOMETHING LIKE THIS? THAT'S A RARE SKILL, MY FRIEND.

GURRR.

GRAGGHH!

SLIP

EASY, BIG FELLA. WE'LL FIX IT.

AND YOU'LL FEEL A LOT BETTER WITH SOME FOOD INSIDE YOU.

SO, WHAT'S CHANGED EXACTLY?

...?!?!

B-DING

SAVED BY THE BELL.

THAT BUYS YOU TIME TO HAVE A LITTLE THINK.

GIRL, WHAT HAVE YOU DONE *NOW?*

I should've listened to your advice. Now I think I've made things worse...

TODAY 19:38

TROUBLE?

EVIE'S PROMISED TO BE LIONEL'S PROM DATE IN RETURN FOR SOME HELP WITH HER LAPTOP.

B-DING

SAYS SHE COULDN'T HELP HERSELF.

B-DING

APPARENTLY HE'S JUST TEXTED TO SAY HE HAS SOMETHING TO TELL HER.

TAKATAKA

CH-CH-TAK

LIONEL IS BESOTTED, BUT WAY OUT OF HIS DEPTH.

IT ISN'T THE ONLY FANTASY RELATIONSHIP ON HER MIND RIGHT NOW.

SHE HAS TO PUT LIONEL OUT OF HIS MISERY... AND NOW IS THE TI--

I'VE JUST WORKED OUT WHAT'S DIFFERENT ABOUT YOU... NEW NAIL COLOUR, RIGHT?

NO, WAIT -- YOUR EYEBROWS ARE DARKER!

THE LAST THING I NEEDED RIGHT NOW WAS DISTRACTION.

Just trying to find the right words to bail from the date. Between us, Lionel makes me feel suffocated, but I can't be that brutal

TODAY 19:42

MALLO

REPLY

Have you done the deed?

TODAY 19:40

LIONEL

EPLY   DELE

TAP

THUMB

TAP

WITH MALLORY OUT OF THE WAY, IT WAS TIME TO DO THE RIGHT THING...

SEN

B-DING

ALL I HAD TO DO WAS FIND THE RIGHT WORDS.

OH, LEAVE ME ALONE!

HOW COULD YOU DO THIS TO ME, EVIE?

♪ DIDDLE DAH DAH ♪ ♪ DIDDLE DAH... ♪

FWOOSH

KRIK

YOU *USED* ME! AFTER EVERYTHING I TRIED TO DO FOR YOU...

WELL, WHATEVER YOU WERE HOPING I COULD FIX, IT ISN'T A PROBLEM ANY MORE!

DELETED

LIONEL, WHAT ARE YOU NOW? A VICTIM OR A VANDAL?

≎PHEW!≎ OK. THE ORIGINAL VERSION IS STILL THERE. WHATEVER THOSE UPDATES WERE TRYING TO PATCH SHE CAN FIGURE IT OUT HERSELF.

I'VE GOT BETTER THINGS TO DO WITH MY LIFE!

E.SCAPE

F34301E

G7959R

J5UGG

L0957Q

M4933A

GATEWAY.exe

GATEWAY UPDATES

EMPTY

HERE'S YOUR LAPTOP. FIND SOMEONE 'LESS SUFFOCATING' TO FIX YOUR APP!

PLEASE DON'T WALK AWAY, LIONEL, I FEEL TERRIBLE...

I KNOW YOU'RE ANGRY, AND I'M SORRY...

SLAM

WHAT I DID WAS UNFORGIVABLE. I'M JUST BEGGING YOU FOR A CHANCE –

JUST ME, OR IS IT HARD TO BREATHE IN HERE?

54

LIONEL WAS SO KIND, AND I HAD CRUSHED HIM.

ALL I WANTED TO DO WAS LOCK MY BEDROOM DOOR AND HIDE AWAY.

AND THAT MADE THE DESIRE TO RETURN TO E.SCAPE ALL THE MORE INTENSE.

JOE & CASPAR
HIT THE ROAD

JUST THEN, I FELT SHUT OUT FROM BOTH WORLDS.

I FIGURED A MOMENT LOOKING IN ON MY LOST PARADISE WOULD HELP ME TO FEEL BETTER.

CLICK

A BROKEN CONNECTION.
THAT'S ALL I EXPECTED...

... BUT THEN MY SENSES
TOOK ME BY SURPRISE.

... AND FEEL SUNSHINE
ON MY FACE.

I COULD BREATHE THE
AIR, HEAR BIRDSONG
ON THE BREEZE ...

WHATEVER LIONEL HAD
DONE TO THE APP...

PART TWO

SO, OUR MAIN MEAL IS SORTED, AND I'M HAPPY TO COOK, WHICH LEAVES JUST TWO TASKS ON THE LIST.

YOU'RE IN CHARGE OF DESSERT...

... AND WASHING UP.

OK, SO I'LL WASH UP AFTERWARDS.

SOME FRUIT WOULD BE GOOD, CHIEF.

SEEING THAT YOU CAN REACH SO MUCH HIGHER THAN ME, IT MAKES SENSE FOR YOU TO DO IT.

WE MIGHT BE ALONE IN THIS WORLD, BUT WE'LL ALWAYS HAVE EACH OTHER... AND DESSERT.

WHAT ELSE DO WE NEED?

I'D LONGED TO RETURN TO E.SCAPE FOR AGES. THE MOMENT I ARRIVED, THERE WAS JUST ONE PLACE I WANTED TO BE.

IN A WORLD IN BLOOM ONCE MORE, FLOWERING FROM THE RUINS OF THE LAST, I WASN'T SURE WHAT I'D FIND WHEN I REACHED MY DESTINATION.

BUT EVERY STEP OF THE WAY, I CLUNG TO THE HOPE THAT IT WOULD HELP ME FIND WHAT I WAS LOOKING FOR.

AND THAT STARTED WITH A CHANCE TO FEEL CLOSE TO MY DAD ONCE MORE.

THE LAST TIME WE SAID GOODBYE, I SENSED IT WAS FOR GOOD. I COULD JUST IMAGINE MY DAD HITTING THE SWITCH TO REBOOT THIS WORLD, KNOWING HIS DAUGHTER WAS SAFELY HOME, AND THEN STEPPING OUTSIDE FOR ONE LAST LOOK.

SO, I DIDN'T EXPECT TO FIND HIM HERE. BUT AS THIS WAS THE HEART OF HIS VIRTUAL CREATION, BURIED IN THE HEART OF A MOUNTAIN, IT SEEMED LIKE THE RIGHT PLACE TO COME.

IT WAS A CHANCE TO GATHER MY THOUGHTS, CONSIDER MY NEXT STEPS... AND TAKE IN WHAT DAD HAD LEFT FOR ME.

February 22nd 2002

I'm a good man at heart, but I've done a very bad thing. As a result, my dear wife is lost in a virtual wilderness, and I must face the consequences. Every day, I look at our daughter and see my reflection in her eyes: a fool guilty of placing too much faith in technology. Now that Evie can speak, she sometimes asks after her mother. In response I show her pictures from a happier time. She's too young to know the truth.

February 27th 2002

The gateway into e.scape is the problem. The original build just wasn't ready. I had been so focused on patching the code to prevent digital natives from slipping into our world that I neglected to realise that it was never primed to let humans return. The update successfully locked out unwanted visitors as planned, but now my dear wife has crossed over and we've all paid a terrible price. I just hope the key is close at hand.

March 30th 2002

Every update I code to unlock the gateway ends in failure and despair! I can't even restore a visual connection, just so we can see each other again. Meanwhile, our beautiful daughter is denied her mother. But I refuse to give up on my family. We will be together some day. I have to make it happen.

October 31st 2003

On many occasions, I've thought about crossing into e.scape in search of my sweetheart. Even with no chance of returning, it's a powerful draw. Then I consider our little girl, and know that her mother would insist I remain at her side. Yes, I could take Evie with me, but what future would she face in a virtual wilderness? This world was intended as a break from reality, not a sentence without end. All I can do is be a good father, while devoting my life to pursuing a fix for this terrible mistake I've made.

December 24th 2003

The festive season is upon us once again. Unlike the last dark years, I'm hoping the surprise I have in store will light up Evie's life. For I've created a chat interface that might just connect us to her mum. It's a long shot, but I can only think that every day my wife must return to the place where she arrived in escape - hoping to come home. The virtual laptop she'll find there won't bring her back just yet. Even so, she can open up a message window on my screen so we can chat - and take comfort in the fact that we're with her in spirit.

March 7th, 2004

Another year and this nightmare continues. The message window is permanently open on my screen. I dream of the moment that letters and words appear as she types them from her virtual keyboard. I am ready to reply, but the cursor just blinks and blinks - marking every second of this seemingly endless sentence that keeps us apart.

September 13th 2005

Evie started school this week. I'm so proud of her (even if she did get on the wrong bus on her first day) and know her mum would feel the same way. When I'm not working on the gateway, I find myself blending photographs of how our daughter looks today with images of me and her mother from our time together. Some are so good that for a moment I'm convinced they're real. It comes as a comfort, until my attention returns to the accursed code. I will crack this!

April 9th 2006

'Is she dead?' asked Evie yesterday, which took me completely by surprise. I couldn't answer her for tears, which told her everything I would wish her to know right now.

May 27th, 2009

Technology has transformed our lives, and yet it continues to taunt me. The latest upgrade to the gateway opens up the return path for human visitors, but only for the blink of an eye. I am close, but not close enough. The struggle continues...

September 8th, 2013

Today, our daughter officially becomes a teenager! I considered telling her everything, but couldn't bring myself to do so. She seemed so happy, with everything to live for. Just watching her prepare to blow out the candles on her cake was enough to remind me what I had to do. As she made a wish, I hoped that before her next birthday she would have someone very special at her side.

February 6th 2014

I haven't been myself for some time. I am tired, with constant heartburn, and put this down to my endless quest. Today, however, my doctor asked me to be seated, and broke the news that I should make the most of what little time I had left. My time is up, it seems, but I could think of just one thing I had to do. Strikingly, I felt no fear about what I faced, just sadness at what we had missed as a family. And so I returned home more determined than ever before to make up for my mistakes.

October 31st 2014

I am weak but elated! After years of torment, my latest update to the gateway has worked! At last, the software now permits a human visitor to come and go at will, while preventing any digital native from trespassing. At first I expected my dear wife to seize the opportunity to come home, but many years have passed since I lost her. Even if she's turned her back on that laptop, I still have every intention of tracking her down so she can return. While the system is stable, and backed up on a portable hard drive for good measure, there's one last thing I must do before my work is truly done. Then, I can rest in the knowledge that I've taken care of Evie's future despite the mistakes of my past.

June 17th, 2015

Evie knows I'm dying now. I can't hide that from her any more. Even so, she's determined that life at home goes on as normal, which is exactly as I wish it to be. I'll always be with her in spirit, just as I am with her mother. And soon I hope the time will come when Evie feels closer to us both. I have now recorded instructions that will guide her to e.scape when she's ready. There, in a realm programmed to reflect her personality, she will find a sanctuary. A place to rest and recharge so she might make the most of her life in the real world.

$$\int d^2$$

September 10th, 2015

Until now I've always kept this journal safely tucked away under the water tank in the loft. Evie will read it one day, no doubt, but that has to be in the right time and place. And so, having stashed the portable hard drive in my favourite hiding place (for I'm no longer a man who takes risks), I now find myself facing the webcam with the book in my lap. The undertaking has exhausted me, but I'm ready at last to make my final journey. I've left instructions for Evie, but I won't say goodbye. Why? Because we will see each other again.

I just hope that I can say the same thing about my poor, beloved wife. For she has to be out there somewhere - adrift in a virtual world - awaiting a connection.

Final update

Time moves differently here in e.scape. It feels like I have been here for an eternity, and yet I know the end is near. Evie has arrived, but a corrupting influence followed her. No doubt her cousin, Mallory, will change for the better on their return, but it leaves me to take drastic digital measures. We've said our goodbyes, and in a moment from now I must wipe all life from the surface of e.scape in order to reboot it. Even if it means letting go of those she found here, my final wish is that my daughter might come back one day - and find the sun shining again.

For with light, there is hope. And should you find yourself reading these last words of mine, Evie, maybe you will understand why I never gave in to darkness.

Dad X

MY MUM IS ALIVE...

... NOT JUST ALIVE BUT POSSIBLY STILL HERE IN E.SCAPE?!

OH, DAD. WHY DIDN'T YOU TELL ME ALL THIS?

MAYBE THIS IS THE ONLY WAY HE COULD EVER SHARE IT.

!?!

UNITY! WHERE ARE YOU?

I'M HERE TO WELCOME YOU BACK, EVIE; TO PROVIDE COMFORT AND GUIDANCE.

THAT'S HOW YOUR FATHER PROGRAMMED ME.

IT'S BEEN A LONG TIME, NO?

APART FROM THE TEARS, YOU'RE LOOKING GOOD! NOW, WHY DON'T YOU GIVE ME A HUG?

BUT... BUT HOW? WHERE ARE YOU?

A MOMENT LATER, DESPITE EVERYTHING THAT HAD GONE WRONG, I WAS REMINDED WHY DAD FIRST CREATED THIS WORLD FOR ME.

YOU'RE NEVER ALONE IN E.SCAPE, EVIE. NEVER ALONE...

...AND ALWAYS LOVED.

LOVE HAS KIND OF MESSED ME UP LATELY. FOR A START, I'VE SPENT ALL YEAR THINKING ABOUT SOMEONE BEYOND MY REACH.

YOU'RE TALKING ABOUT A POWERFUL CONNECTION. LOVE CAN EXIST ACROSS TIME AND SPACE, BUT THAT FEELING IN YOUR HEART HAS TO BE **SHARED** FOR YOU TO THRIVE.

WELL, AFTER EVERYTHING I'VE READ, I HAVE TO ACCEPT HE'S GONE FOR GOOD.

ONLY NOW IT SEEMS THE MOTHER I THOUGHT I'D LOST SO LONG AGO COULD WELL BE OUT HERE SOMEWHERE.

THEN YOU DID THE RIGHT THING BY COMING BACK. 'WITH LIGHT THERE IS HOPE,' RIGHT?

HE HAD MUM IN MIND WHEN HE WROTE THAT. NOW I'M HERE AGAIN AND THE SUN IS SHINING.

I HAVE TO LOOK FOR HER, UNITY.

EVEN IF I FIND NOTHING, IT'S WHAT HE WOULD'VE WANTED.

AND IT'S WHAT I WANT JUST AS MUCH.

WHATEVER IT TAKES, EVIE, I'LL BE AT YOUR SIDE EVERY STEP OF THE WAY.

YOUR FATHER MADE THE ULTIMATE SACRIFICE WHEN HE RESET THIS WORLD.

HE KNEW HE WOULDN'T SEE IT REGENERATE, BUT IT MUST BE COMFORTING TO KNOW THAT HE BELIEVED YOU'D COME BACK AND FINISH HIS SEARCH.

BUT DAD WIPED OUT EVERYTHING ON THE SURFACE OF E.SCAPE. IT WAS THE ONLY WAY TO STOP THE CORRUPTION FROM SPREADING.

HE SAID SO HIMSELF.

IF MUM REALLY WAS HERE, SURELY SHE'S GONE NOW?

WITH LIGHT...

... THERE IS HOPE. I KNOW THAT NOW.

WHERE WOULD YOU BE WITHOUT IT?

BACK IN MY BEDROOM MOST LIKELY...

... FEELING SORRY FOR MYSELF NO DOUBT.

AND NOW YOU'RE BACK, THANKS TO YOUR FATHER, WITH A CHANCE TO MAKE SENSE OF YOUR FEELINGS.

THIS IS A JOURNEY OF DISCOVERY, EVIE. WHATEVER HAPPENS, I GUARANTEE YOU'LL LEARN MORE ABOUT YOURSELF ALONG THE WAY THAN STEWING ON THINGS AT HOME.

UNITY, AS MUCH AS I APPRECIATE YOUR WISE WORDS, I'M JUST PLEASED YOU'RE HERE...

... AND HOPE YOU KNOW YOUR WAY AROUND THESE SCREENS.

IF MUM IS HERE, SHE'LL SHOW UP SOMEWHERE...

YOUR FATHER TAUGHT ME EVERYTHING ABOUT HIS CREATION.

NATURALLY.

WE COULD BE DOING THIS FOR SOME TIME, COULDN'T WE?

YEP.

≠SIGH≠

YOU JUST HAVE TO BE PATIENT.

OR LOOK AT THINGS IN A DIFFERENT WAY?

...?

ALL THIS TIME, I THOUGHT MUM HAD PASSED AWAY. NOW I SEE THINGS FROM A NEW PERSPECTIVE, AND YOU KNOW WHAT? AS MUCH AS IT HURTS, I UNDERSTAND WHY DAD KEPT THINGS FROM ME.

SAY NO MORE, EVIE. I KNOW WHERE THIS IS GOING.

IT'S ALL ABOUT THE BIGGER PICTURE, RIGHT?

MASTER CAMERA

OVERGROUND

FOR ONCE, I HAD A CHANCE TO APPRECIATE MY DAD'S LIFE WORK.

I JUST COULDN'T IMAGINE THE TORMENT HE HAD PUT HIMSELF THROUGH, KNOWING THAT MUM WAS TRAPPED IN A MIRACLE OF HIS CREATION.

I COULD ONLY THINK HE'D SCOURED THIS LAND AS WE WERE NOW:

HOLDING OUT HOPE AGAINST ALL ODDS, BUT ENDING UP WITH NOTHING.

IF ANYONE KNEW HOW TO LOOK AT THINGS DIFFERENTLY, IT WAS DAD.

HE WAS A DEEP THINKER ALRIGHT.

UNITY, *THAT'S IT!* ONCE HE'D CHECKED OUT EVERY PIXEL ON THE SURFACE, MY DAD WOULDN'T HAVE STOPPED THERE.

YOUR FATHER NEVER GAVE UP, FOR SURE.

EXACTLY! HE'D SIMPLY TAKE THINGS TO ANOTHER LEVEL!

WHAT'S MORE, IF I WAS MUM, THERE'S ONLY ONE THING I'D DO WHEN LIFE STACKED UP AGAINST ME.

LOCK YOURSELF AWAY IN YOUR BEDROOM?

IN A SENSE, YES...

OVERGROUND

UNDERGROUND

I'M TALKING ABOUT GOING TO GROUND.

81

...?

SEE FOR YOURSELF.

DOES THAT LOOK FAMILIAR TO YOU?

WHAT THE --

LOOKS LIKE DAD WAS BUSY WHILE YOU WERE OUT THERE SEEKING WISDOM AND ENLIGHTENMENT.

THE ENTRANCE!

THE ONLY WAY IS DOWN, IT SEEMS.

MALLORY, GO AND TELL YOUR COUSIN HER SUPPER IS ON THE TABLE. SHE CAN'T GO TO PROM NIGHT HUNGRY.

EVIE DOESN'T HAVE A DATE. SHE'LL HAVE PLENTY OF TIME TO FILL UP ON BUFFET SNACKS LATER. WHAT ELSE IS SHE GOING TO BE DOING?

DO AS YOUR MOTHER ASKS. NOW, MALLORY...

BUT I'M ON A TIGHT SCHEDULE HERE. I NEED TO EAT AND THEN DO MY NAILS.

MAL!!!

UNBELIEVABLE!

OI! EVIE! DINNER IS ON THE TABLE!

SHE SAYS SHE'S ON HER WAY. AT LEAST I IMAGINE SHE DID. MOST PROBABLY GOT HER EARPLUGS IN –

– HAVING A LITTLE CRY TO HERSELF.

EVIE?

CLICK

YOU CAN'T FOOL ME, MADAM.

SNEAKING OUT TO PROM IN A DRESS I'D DISAPPROVE OF, NO DOUBT.

SSSHUT

MALLORY, YOU'RE NOT LEAVING TONIGHT UNTIL I'VE VETTED YOUR OUTFIT. I WANT TO SEE A HEMLINE NO HIGHER THAN THE KNEES.

... WHAT??

IN DARKNESS, THIS DEEP DOWN, WE SOON LOST TRACK OF TIME...

SQUEEEE

SQUEEE

SQUEE

SQUEEEE

SQUEEE

SQUEEE

... AND ANY SENSE OF JUST HOW FAR WE'D TRAVELLED.

SQUEEE

WHERE ARE YOU, MY FRIEND? I MEAN, HOW LONG DOES IT TAKE TO FORAGE FOR FRUIT? WE'RE HARDLY TALKING ABOUT A HUNTING EXPEDITION HERE.

OAK?

HOW CAN SOMETHING SO BIG BE THIS HARD TO FIND?

=SIGH=

HMM...

... HUH?

I'VE SEEN THIS BEFORE. IN ANOTHER LIFE, PERHAPS?

... OAK?

WHAT HAS HAPPENED HERE?

COME BACK, WHEREVER YOU ARE.

BLINK

BLINK

... HUH?

BLINK

E CAPE

BLINK

G7959R

BLING

L0957Q

BLANK

M4933A

GATEWAY.exe

BLINK

EMPTY

BLINK

BLINK

BLINK

SO WHOSE BRIGHT IDEA WAS IT TO WALK TO THE BIGGEST EVENT OF THE YEAR?

MY FEET ARE KILLING ME IN THESE HEELS.

OH, I KNOW... MY BOYFRIEND!

LIMOS ARE FOR LOSERS, BABE. NOBODY CARES HOW YOU GOT HERE. WHAT MATTERS IS THE ENTRANCE YOU'RE ABOUT TO MAKE.

THIS IS US, REMEMBER? THIS YEAR'S GUARANTEED PROM KING AND QUEEN.

MALLORY AND JASPAR.

THAT'S JALLORY... NO, MASPAR.

NOT TONIGHT IT ISN'T. UNLESS YOU INCLUDE YOU KNOW WHO...

WELL, LET ME SEE. LIONJALLORY ROLLS OFF THE TONGUE.

DID YOU HAVE TO BRING HIM ALONG WITH US?

EVIE LET HIM DOWN BADLY.

THE NEW MALLORY TAKES CARE OF THE HOPELESS CASES.

JASIONORY... LASPOREL...

BUT HE'LL CLING TO ME LIKE A LIMPET. WHAT WILL PEOPLE THINK?

JASPAR, LOVE ME, LOVE THE LOSERS IN MY COUSIN'S LIFE. THAT'S THE DEAL.

MALLSPARNEL! TOTALLY NAILS IT.

WHERE IS EVIE ANYWAY?

WELL, I CHECKED OUR FRIDGE AND SHE ISN'T IN THERE...

... SO I CAN ONLY THINK SHE'S FOUND A WARMER PLACE TO HIDE OUT UNTIL THIS WHOLE SHAME STORM BLOWS OVER.

ALL YOU HAVE TO DO NOWADAYS IS PRESS ONE WRONG BUTTON AND **BOOM** -- YOUR WORLD TURNS INSIDE OUT.

ON THE UPSIDE, THANK GOODNESS IT DIDN'T HAPPEN TO ME.

JASPONEL--

LIONEL, DON'T EVER SHIP MY NAME WITH YOURS, OK?

WE'RE **UNSHIPPABLE.**

OK, BOYS, RUN
AND HOLD THE HA
OPEN FOR ME. IF
SHOW UP WITHOU
YOU HAD BETTE
THIS MEMOR

SHRIEEKK!!!

WHAT
IS THAT
THING?!

SOMEONE
CALL THE
POLICE!

JUST TAKE MY
PURSE BUT DON'T
HURT ME!

KLANG

MURRGHHH!

KLUP

SPR LNG

WHUMP

≥WHIMPER≤

STAY COOL, UNITY. WE'VE COME TOO FAR TO TURN AROUND NOW.

YOU MUST FORGIVE MY LACK OF COURAGE. I EXIST TO WELCOME YOU INTO THIS WORLD, AND YET HERE WE ARE UNDERNEATH THE SURFACE IN A REALM I NEVER KNEW EXISTED.

PLUS THESE TORCHES WON'T LAST MUCH LONGER. WE'LL NEVER FIND OUR WAY BACK IF THEY GO OUT.

I'M KIND OF USED TO DARK TIMES, UNITY. IN A WEIRD WAY, I FEEL RIGHT AT HOME!

NOW, IF YOU WANT TO TURN AROUND THAT'S FINE, BUT I'M NOT STOPPING NOW.

IF THERE'S A CHANCE THAT MY MUM IS DOWN HERE SOMEWHERE, I HAVE TO KEEP LOOKING.

I CAN'T REST UNTIL I'VE FINISHED THIS SEARCH.

THERE IS LIGHT, EVIE.

DAD'S WORDS GOT US DOWN HERE ALL RIGHT, BUT THEY'RE NOT GOING TO HELP US SEE ANYTHING WHEN THESE TORCHES DIE.

IT'S OK TO BE SCARED, UNITY.

NO, I MEAN THERE REALLY IS LIGHT. OVER THERE. *LOOK!*

UNITY WAS WARY, BUT I DIDN'T WANT TO SHOW MY TRUE FEELINGS IN CASE IT MADE THINGS WORSE.

SPLOOSH

SPLOOSH

SPLISH

I COULDN'T AFFORD TO BE AFRAID OF THE DARK OR THE UNKNOWN, BUT ONE THING TERRIFIED ME – THAT ALL THIS MIGHT COME TO NOTHING.

I JUST HAD TO BELIEVE THAT MY DAD WASN'T CHASING A DREAM TO MAKE UP FOR THE NIGHTMARE HE HAD CREATED FOR HIMSELF. IF I STARTED TO DOUBT THAT MUM WAS DOWN HERE SOMEWHERE, MY COURAGE WOULD QUICKLY DESERT ME.

BRING IT IN QUIETLY, UNITY.

SPLOOSH

SKREEEP

SORRY!

102

RIGHT NOW I SHOULD BE REVELLING IN THE SOLITUDE AND SILENCE.

BUT THE FACT IS I FEEL LIKE WE'RE BEING WATCHED.

STAY STRONG, UNITY. STAY STRONG AND STAY FOCUSED.

IN TRUTH I SENSED IT, TOO...

JUST THINK HAPPY THOUGHTS AND WE'LL BE FINE.

WE WEREN'T ALONE.

FFT FFT

NOTHING BAD CAN HAPPE-- OW!

YELP!

ALL I COULD DO WAS CLING TO HOPE.

EVEN AS THE LIGHT WENT OUT.

PART THREE

SO, I HAD LOST A FRIEND...

... BUT I WOULD FIND HIM.

!?!

VRROOOOM

HONK

EVEN IF I HAD TO GO TO THE ENDS OF A STRANGE, HOSTILE WORLD.

HAHA! HAHA! HA! HAHAHA!

HA! HA!

OK, THAT'S ENOUGH.

I SAID THAT'S ENOUGH!

FOR ALL WE KNOW, THIS PAIR COULD BE SCOUTS AHEAD OF A TOPSIDE INVASION!

ARLO, GUARD THEM WITH YOUR LIFE WHILE I RAISE THE ALARM.

WHOA! REALLY?

THAT JUST MEANS YOU DON'T MESS UP, ALRIGHT?

GOT IT, KNOX. YOU CAN RELY ON ME.

117

OK, HE'S GONE. TIME OUT, MY FRIENDS!

THESE GUYS AREN'T GOING ANYWHERE.

BESIDES, KNOX IS ALL MOUTH.

HEH HEH!

UNITY, D'YOU HEAR ME? THESE KIDS ARE CRAZY. WE COULD BE IN TROUBLE HERE!

WHAT HAPPENED?

I'M MORE CONCERNED ABOUT WHAT *MIGHT* HAPPEN IF WE HANG AROUND ANY LONGER.

THIS GANG IS ARMED, KIND OF WILD, AND CLEARLY IN NEED OF LETTING OFF STEAM.

THAT'S NOT A GOOD COMBINATION AMONG THE YOUTH.

THEN LET'S GET OUT OF HERE WHILE WE HAVE THE CHANCE.

EASY NOW. DON'T MAKE A SOUND.

SPLASH

WOOO

SPLOOSH

SHRIEK

WHAT IS GOING ON HERE?

119

IT'S ME. EVIE! YOUR DAUGHTER...

?!?

... EVIE?

I CAN SEE SO MUCH OF ME IN YOU.

YOU HAVE THE SAME EYES.

THE SAME VOICE.

THE SAME HEART.

THE SAME SOUL.

A LONG TIME AGO YOU RISKED EVERYTHING TO SAVE ME. I'M HERE TO DO THE SAME FOR YOU.

BUT I DON'T NEED SAVING.

...?

HERE WAS MY MOTHER...

... A WOMAN I HAD NEVER DREAMED THAT I WOULD MEET...

... AND YET SHE SEEMED SO... DISTANT.

GROWING UP, I USED TO TREASURE DAD'S MEMORIES OF MY MOTHER. I HAD NO REASON TO CONSIDER WHAT SHE HAD BECOME.

EVIE, PERHAPS WE SHOULD LEAVE?

OK, IT'S TIME WE TURNED OUR ATTENTION TO FOOD. WHO IS ON FOOD GATHERING DUTY?

SHE WAS A DETERMINED WOMAN, ALL RIGHT.

I COULDN'T IMAGINE HOW TOUGH IT MUST'VE BEEN FOR MUM TO EMBRACE HER NEW LIFE HERE. ALL I KNEW WAS THAT IT HAD CHANGED HER.

NOW I'D BEEN GIVEN THIS CHANCE, AND IT FELT LIKE COMING FACE TO FACE WITH A STRANGER. WE HAD BOTH MOVED ON, I REALISED. TWO SURVIVORS LIVING DIFFERENT LIVES.

IT WAS TIME TO GO HOME.

WILL YOU DO ONE LAST THING FOR ME?

...?

WHEN I FACE THE WEBCAM, I'D LIKE YOU TO BE AT MY SIDE. IT'LL FEEL LIKE A PROPER GOODBYE.

BUT THAT MEANS SURFACING.

I HAVEN'T BEEN TOPSIDE FOR YEARS.

IT'S A WHOLE NEW WORLD UP THERE. TRUST ME, I'VE SEEN IT.

YOU MIGHT BE PLEASANTLY SURPRISED!

=SIGH=

=SNIFF=

HOWL

KLANG
KLUP

MURGGHH?

KLANG
KLUP KLUP

THE LENGTHS I GO TO SAVE YOUR SKIN...

BUDDY, YOU'D BETTER BE READY TO CARRY ME HOME AFTER THIS. MY FEET ARE *SORE*.

GRAAGH-HOO!!

WELL, THAT WASN'T THERE WHEN I ARRIVED!

SOMEONE'S BEEN HERE.

BEEN AND GONE BY THE LOOK OF THINGS.

BUT THE GATEWAY'S SECURE NOW. DAD'S FINAL UPDATE FIXED EVERYTHING.

THAT MIGHT BE SO...

E.SCAPE

F34301E

G7959P

BUT THE PROGRAM CONTAINS NO UPDATES. EVEN THE FIRST ONE THAT TRAPPED ME HERE IS MISSING. THIS IS THE ORIGINAL GATEWAY, EVIE...

GATEWAY.exe

GATEWAY UPDATES

EMPTY

... THE ONE THAT ALLOWS THE DIGITAL NATIVES TO SLIP THROUGH.

BUT STOPS US FROM GOING HOME. DAD WROTE ABOUT IT IN HIS JOURNAL.

CAN THIS BE SABOTAGE?

ONLY ONE PERSON HAD ACCESS TO THE CODE, BUT HE'D NEVER DO SUCH A THING. NOT DELIBERATELY. I'M NOT EVEN SURE HE KNEW WHAT HE WAS DOING WHEN HE TRIED TO FIX IT, WHICH MEANS...

... OH.

OK, SO NOBODY SABOTAGED THE SOFTWARE... BUT SOMEONE MIGHT'VE MESSED UP.

BOSS, OVER HERE...

WHATEVER WENT THROUGH IS MASSIVE.

IT'S A BRUTE, MA'AM. MAKE NO MISTAKE.

THOSE AVATARS ARE PROGRAMMED TO PACK A PUNCH.

LET ME TAKE CARE OF THIS. I CAN BRING IT BACK.

OUT OF THE QUESTION.

?!?

NOT ONLY IS A BRUTE CAPABLE OF CRUSHING ANYONE IN ITS PATH, THERE'S NO WAY YOU CAN GO AFTER IT NOW. WITHOUT THE LATEST UPDATE, THIS GATEWAY PREVENTS HUMANS FROM RETURNING.

SO, ONLY THE AVATARS CAN CROSS OVER?

MY HUNTERS WILL TAKE CARE OF THIS. IF THERE'S A BRUTE ON THE LOOSE IN REALITY, THEY'LL BRING IT BACK...

... DEAD OR ALIVE.

OAK, YOU HAVE TO PROMISE ME ONE THING.

GUH?

IF ANYONE FREAKS OUT ON YOU HERE YOU WON'T FREAK OUT ON THEM, OK?

I KNOW YOU'RE A PUSSYCAT ON THE INSIDE, BUT THESE PEOPLE ARE QUICK TO JUDGE ON LOOKS ALONE.

MURGGHH!?

I KNOW. IT'S NOT A WORLD THAT MAKES MUCH SENSE TO ME EITHER.

ALTHOUGH I CAN UNDERSTAND WHY THEY'D WANT TO LIFT THEIR SPIRITS IN THIS WAY. REALITY CAN BE A COLD, DARK PLACE, IT SEEMS.

GRAWWWL...

WITH A LITTLE MORE SUNSHINE IN THEIR LIVES THERE'D BE NO NEED TO GET AWAY IN THE FIRST PLACE, BUT THAT'S NOT OUR CONCERN.

NOW STAY OUT OF SIGHT AND DON'T MOVE UNTIL I CALL YOU...

DMF DMF BIP DMF BIP BIP DMF

OI! OI! GET IN!

I LOVE THIS CHOON!

WELL, I THINK THAT WENT OK.

THREE PHONE NUMBERS IS NOT A BAD HAUL FOR A FIRST ATTEMPT.

WATCHING YOU STEP IT UP JUST THEN WAS A THING OF BEAUTY, LIONEL. THOSE GIRLS **ADORED** YOU, AND THE PHOTOS I TOOK WERE MADE TO GO VIRAL.

IT'S CERTAINLY GIVEN ME AN APPETITE, I'LL SAY THAT!

FINALLY...

IS THAT WHO I THINK IT IS?

MAYBE.

I HAVE TO GO.

EVIE
CHAT MESSAGE RECEIVED

...can't get home without the update. It's stored on a portable hard drive, taped under the water tank in my old cottage.

Mallory, I'm relying on you! E XXX

WHERE? AT LEAST LET ME FINISH MY SANDWICH.

MALLORY, WAIT!

SO, THIS IS ABOUT EVIE! WHERE IS SHE, MALLORY?

SHE CAN'T HAVE MISSED THE PROM JUST BECAUSE OF ME. C'MON. I WANT TO HELP!

WHAT'S GOING ON?

LEAVE IT, LIONEL.

IT'S A FAMILY THING.

IS THERE ANOTHER GUY? BE HONEST WITH ME, MAL.

IT'S MORE COMPLICATED THAN THAT.

EVIE IS INVOLVED WITH....

... ANOTHER WORLD.

?!

SHE'S TALKING ABOUT A PLACE I CALL HOME.

WHAT THE...? YOU!

BUT I CAN'T GET BACK WITHOUT YOUR HELP.

THIS IS A PRIVATE CONVERSATION, PAL.

DON'T HIT ME.

IT'S OK, LIONEL. HE'S ONE OF THE GOOD GUYS.

YOU MAKE IT SOUND LIKE THERE ARE BAD GUYS OUT THERE.

ACCORDING TO EVIE, THERE COULD BE LOTS OF THEM HERE AT ANY MOMENT, WHICH IS WHY SHE NEEDS MY HELP.

SO, IT SEEMS THAT WE AREN'T THE ONLY VISITORS TO HAVE CROSSED OVER.

CROSSED OVER FROM WHERE?

WHO'S 'WE?'

UM... CAN YOU GUYS KEEP A SECRET?

OAK? IT'S ALRIGHT, BUDDY. YOU CAN SHOW YOURSELF.

SO, WHAT ARE WE LOOKING FOR HERE? A KITTEN?

OMG!

OK, NOT A KITTEN.

THE LAST TIME EVIE AND I SAW ONE OF THOSE, IT WAS KINDA FURIOUS.

THIS IS OAK. YOU HAVE MY WORD THAT HE'S HARMLESS.

AND HARD TO HIDE, RIGHT?

ALL I WANT TO DO IS GET HIM HOME.

LIONEL, SEEING THAT YOU'RE ALL ABOUT PUSHING BOUNDARIES TONIGHT, I NEED YOU TO COLLECT A HARD DRIVE FROM MY COUSIN'S OLD COTTAGE.

BUT OTHER PEOPLE LIVE THERE NOW...

THEN TAKE IT TO EVIE'S BEDROOM - WITHOUT ALERTING MY PARENTS BECAUSE YOU DON'T WANT TO LOOK LIKE A CREEP - AND UPLOAD THE FILE TO HER LAPTOP.

MAL, UM, ARE YOU CRAZY?

NEENAH NEE NA

UNLESS YOU TRY, WE MIGHT NEVER SEE EVIE AGAIN.

?!?

THINGS MIGHT NOT HAVE WORKED OUT BETWEEN YOU, BUT SHE'D DO ANYTHING FOR YOU AS A FRIEND.

WHAT ABOUT YOU?

THESE GUYS NEED A FRIEND, TOO.

"THE HARD DRIVE'S TAPED UNDER THE WATER TANK IN THE LOFT...

... YOU'LL BE IN AND OUT IN NO TIME."

YEAH, RIGHT. LIKE BREAKING INTO HOUSES IS A BREEZE.

GRRR

OK, SO TALKING TO GIRLS TOOK GUTS, BUT I NEED MORE THAN THAT HERE...

... STARTING WITH A SANDWICH.

THERE YOU GO, BIG BOY. FRESHLY MADE FOR THE SCHOOL PROM.

EVIE, IF YOU COULD SEE ME NOW...

CRASH

THEN I'M NOT A VANDAL, OK? JUST A KID TRYING TO DO THE RIGHT THING FOR A FRIEND.

JASPAR, IF I MEAN ANYTHING TO YOU RIGHT NOW, YOU WON'T FREAK OUT ON ME, OK?

I WANT TO INTRODUCE YOU TO A COUPLE OF FRIENDS.

THEY'RE A LONG WAY FROM HOME, AND NEED A PLACE TO LIE LOW FOR A SHORT WHILE.

LIE LOW? ARE THEY BANK ROBBERS?

JUST BE COOL, OK? PROMISE ME THAT.

BABE, I ALWAYS KEEP IT TOGETHER. YOU KNOW ME.

OK, GUYS, COME IN BEFORE SOMEONE SEES YOU OUT THERE.

THIS IS RIVER.

HE'S FROM A DIGITAL WORLD CREATED BY EVIE'S DAD BEFORE HE DIED.

AND THIS IS OAK.

HE WOULDN'T HURT A FLY.

144

MALLORY'S HOUSE

ISN'T IT QUIET WITHOUT THE GIRLS?

ENJOY IT WHILE IT LASTS. THEY'LL BE BACK SOON, NO DOUBT.

DRAINPIPE, DON'T BE THE ≋PUFF≋ SECOND ONE TO ≋GRUNT≋ LET ME DOWN TONIGHT...

HNGHH!!

KLUP

EVIE, WHEREVER YOU ARE...

...WHATEVER'S GOING ON IN YOUR LIFE...

...AT THIS MOMENT IN TIME...

...I'M HERE FOR YOU.

JUST ABOUT...

SO, THESE WOULD BE THE GATEWAY UPDATES I TRASHED. WHOOPS! WELL...

RESTORE MOST RECENT GATEWAY?

Yes   No

X

E.SCAPE
F34301E
G7959R
JSUGG
L0957Q
M4933A
GATEWAY.exe
GATEWAY UPDATES
EMPTY

... AT LEAST I'M HERE TO CLEAN UP THE MESS.

RESTORING MOST RECENT GATEWAY.

47%

X

E.SCAPE
F34301E
G7959R
JSUGG
L0957Q
M4933A
GATEWAY.exe
GATEWAY UPDATES
EMPTY

COME ON... COME ON...

... EVIE? IS THAT YOU?

EVIE? ARE YOU HOME? WE DIDN'T HEAR YOU COME IN.

!!!

COME ON DOWN, SWEETIE.

JUST ONCE THIS EVENING, I'D LIKE TO LEAVE A HOUSE THROUGH THE FRONT DOOR.

MUM, PLEASE!

AT LEAST LET ME TRY TO SETTLE THIS WITHOUT ANYONE GETTING HURT.

EVIE, I'M ASKING YOU TO WALK AWAY AND PRETEND THIS NEVER HAPPENED!

THAT MIGHT'VE SUITED YOU IN E.SCAPE...

... BUT IF SOMEONE IS AT RISK OF GETTING HURT IN THIS WORLD, THEN WE SHOULD FIGHT TO PROTECT THEM!

WILL THE PAIR OF YOU SLOW DOWN!

I'M DESIGNED FOR MEDITATION, NOT MARATHONS!

JUST GIVE IT UP! WHY ARE YOU SO DETERMINED?

OH, I DON'T KNOW? MAYBE I TAKE AFTER DAD IN TRYING TO DO THE RIGHT THING...

MAYBE I SHOULD'VE KEPT MY DISTANCE.

... AND NEVER GIVING UP HOPE.

HE RAISED YOU WELL. THAT MUCH IS CLEAR.

THEN GIVE ME THIS CHANCE...

OH, MUM!

EVERYONE COME DOWN HERE THIS INSTANT!

KNOX, YOU HAVE DEFIED ME...

JUST THEN, I KNEW THAT NOTHING WOULD COMFORT RIVER. HE HAD LOST A TRUE FRIEND. A SOUL MATE THAT COULDN'T BE REPLACED.

I MIGHT'VE SPENT A LONG TIME LIVING WITH FEELINGS FOR HIM, BUT THAT WAS BASED ON NOTHING MORE THAN A FANTASY.

THIS WAS REAL. AND HEARTBREAKING TO WITNESS.

I'M SO SORRY. IF THERE'S ANYTHING WE CAN DO.

WE TRIED OUR BEST...

NATURALLY, THE STRANGE REPORTS OF A GIANT ON THE LOOSE ACROSS THE CITY WOULD KEEP SOCIAL MEDIA BUSY FOR A WHILE...

... BUT WITH NO EVIDENCE, PEOPLE MOVED ON TO OTHER MATTERS...

... AND LIFE RETURNED TO NORMAL.

THANK YOUs

ONCE AGAIN I'D FIRSTLY LIKE TO THANK YOU READING THIS. IT'S BECAUSE OF YOUR MASSIVE LEVELS OF SUPPORT ON THE FIRST GRAPHIC NOVEL THAT I HAVE BEEN GIVEN THE OPPORTUNITY TO CARRY ON WHAT I LOVE AND PRODUCE THIS SECOND ADVENTURE IN THE USERNAME SERIES. I REALLY HOPE YOU SHARE THIS STORY WITH FRIENDS AND FAMILY AND GET THEM INTO THIS AMAZING GENRE OF STORYTELLING.

THANKS SO MUCH TO BRIONY AND JAMIE AND THE REST OF HODDER. YOU HAVE HONESTLY BEEN SO AMAZING FROM START TO FINISH ON THIS BOOK. LIKE...ACTUALLY FAULTLESS, AND FOR THAT I'M VERY GRATEFUL. I'LL ALWAYS REMEMBER ATTENDING MY FIRST BOOK OF THE YEAR AWARDS WITH YOU AND BEING SO NERVOUS AND OUT MY COMFORT ZONE BUT YOU ALL MADE ME FEEL SO WELCOME AND PART OF THE FAMILY. ALSO...THE HOTEL STILL HASN'T CONTACTED ME ABOUT BREAKING THAT DOOR, OOPS.

THANK YOU TO THE SUGG SQUAD: AMRIT, MATT, JOAQUIN AND MINDY. ONCE AGAIN YOU HAVE ALL BEEN THE BEST TEAM I COULD POSSIBLY WISH FOR, GOING ABOVE AND BEYOND MY EXPECTATIONS OF HOW I IMAGINED THIS SECOND STORY TO BE.

THANK YOU TO LUCY, ALEX AND DOM FOR ALL THE HARD WORK AND PATIENCE...AGAIN. THANKS TO ALL MY FELLOW YOUTUBERS, THE BUTTERCREAM AND MY MATES FROM BACK HOME IN THE SHIRE. YOUR SUPPORT IS EVERYTHING TO ME.

LASTLY THANKS TO MY AMAZING FAMILY. KNOWING THAT YOU'RE ALL WATCHING ME GO ON THIS CRAZY RIDE AND SHARING THESE MOMENTS WITH ME MAKES ME SO HAPPY AND I HOPE (WELL I KINDA KNOW ALREADY AS YOU ALL TELL ME A LOT) THAT YOU'RE PROUD OF ME. YOU'VE ALWAYS ENCOURAGED ME TO BE CREATIVE THROUGHOUT MY LIFE AND FOR THAT I CAN'T THANK YOU ENOUGH. ALSO THANKS AGAIN ZOBO FOR THE BOOT UP THE ARSE TO START A YOUTUBE CHANNEL AND BEGIN THIS MAD LIFE I NOW LIVE. I'M A LUCKY SOD.

P.S. I STILL CAN'T DOWN A PINT.